UNDERSTANDING
All Bible Prophecy

Genesis to Revelation

Frank N. Mitchell

This UNDERSTANDING booklet is part of a series of booklets on key issues of our time on the Reign of Christ at
www.ashiningcityonahill.org
www.reignofchrist.org
All booklets are available at amazon.com

September 2018

UNDERSTANDING
All Bible Prophecy
Genesis to Revelation

Prophecy is probably the most controversial and divisive topic in the Body of Christ today. This should not be the case. Why? First, because all non-Liberal, non-apostate Christians agree on the fundamentals or, that is, the basics or the essentials of the Atonement, the Resurrection, the Virgin Birth, the inspiration and authority of Scripture, and the eventual return of Christ at some point in history with Him coming back in the clouds as He left. (Acts 1:11, 1 Thessalonians 4:16-17)

Further, all Christians should agree but they do not always that we should be working and praying for the Kingdom to come on planet Earth just as Jesus instructed or commanded until He comes back whenever that might be. "Occupy until I come." said Jesus. (Luke 19:13)

Amillennialism
The reason why prophecy becomes important while at the same time being divisive is if one is an amillennialist (that is, no Kingdom come on Earth in all its fullness), there tends to be little or no motivation (outside some rudimentary evangelism and works of charity) to do any serious Kingdom work or any serious praying for the Kingdom to

come on Earth as it is in Heaven. Scripture is quite clear that if one is not working or praying for the Kingdom, one can still possibly go to Heaven (if one is truly trusting in the atoning work of Jesus), but one will have no rewards and one's worthless works will be burned up as wood, hay and stubble. (1 Corinthians 3:12)

However, there are in fact countless prophecies about the Kingdom of God come on Earth in all its fullness that we are supposed to be working and praying for. For these reasons, in my opinion, amillennialism is quite possibly a doctrine of devils meant to render Christians' lives fruitless and ineffective for God and His Kingdom come on Earth.

Premillennialism
Another reason why prophecy becomes important as well as divisive is if one is a premillennialist (that is, Christ returns *before* the Kingdom comes on Earth in all its fullness), there also tends to be little or no motivation to do any serious Kingdom work (again, outside some rudimentary evangelism and works of charity) or any serious praying for the Kingdom to come on Earth as it is in Heaven because it is not going to happen until Jesus comes back. So, forget about it!

Again, there are in fact countless prophecies about the Kingdom of God come on Earth in all its fullness that we are supposed to be working and praying for, and it makes little or no sense to say those prophecies do not happen until Christ physically returns and the dead are raised (to get eternal bodies) and life in this world, in effect, ends as we know it. This would mean there is no reason to be working for the Kingdom to come if it is not going to happen until Jesus comes back and life in this world as we know it ends.   For these reasons, in my opinion, premillennialism is also quite possibly a doctrine of devils meant to render Christians' lives fruitless and ineffective for God.

Further, the wildly popular premillennialist view as it is usually argued has a lot of inconsistencies that are completely ignored by its advocates. First Corinthians 15:52 is crystal clear that the dead are raised "at the last trump" and not at some point in history a thousand years before the last trump. Further, if God gets confused and accidentally does the last trump a thousand years early, as the premillennialist holds, then there will be people running around the Earth in eternal bodies that will not be procreating (said Jesus), and there will be people not in eternal bodies living a life as we know it today. Scripture does not teach anywhere to my knowledge that there is going to be some half-way remade Earth that exists for a thousand before there is "a new heaven and a new earth." of Rev 21:1 and Isaiah 66:22-24 and 2 Peter 3:13.

Further, on more minor points, the premillennialist is not able to connect all the dots in his half-way remade life and world for such a thousand year time on Earth. One of the major prophecies the premillennialist often relies on is in Daniel about 70 weeks (of years) from the order "to restore and build Jerusalem" in Daniel 9:25 to the coming of the Messiah and the Kingdom come on Earth. The accuracy of this prophecy in terms of weeks of years and this interpretation by the premillennialist is debated.

However, I think the premillennialist is correct, and this prophecy has an uncanny accuracy in terms of weeks of years, though it is not clear in reality exactly when the order was given or which of such orders is referred to in the prophecy. Still, having said this, it appears to this writer the premillennialist view is almost certainly true because it talks of a coming Messiah who is cut off for the sins of his people in the middle of the seventieth week of years. These seems to me to be uncontroversially Jesus. However, if the Messiah is cut off for the sins of his people in the middle of the seventieth week of years, this leaves **only** a three and a half year period to be fulfilled when the clock of prophecy starts ticking again, so to speak, in order for the Kingdom to then come on Earth in all its fullness.

Understanding the Book of Revelation
Having only three and a half years left (of the seventy weeks of years in Daniel) becomes a huge problem for the premillennialist who needs an entire seven years yet to play out in the Daniel prophecy in order for the premillennialist to make his theory of

seven years of Revelation tribulation yet to play out. Only having three and a half years seems to completely undo his whole understanding of Revelation, and then his whole seven-year Tribulation construction in Revelation implodes, and it would seem so does all the premillennialism that goes with it.

However, **the more general problem** and in fact mistake that emerges in Revelation for premillennialism is that it tends to take all the figurative symbolism to be physically true concerning fish in the sea and marks of the beast on the hand or forehead or even marks on the saints given by God (a seemingly little known prophecy).

In general, the conservative is correct that the Bible *when at all possible* should be taken as literally true whether dealing with the Resurrection, the Virgin Birth, the Creation, or miracles generally. It is the Liberal who wants, incorrectly, to make everything symbolic or metaphorical or primitive man's superstition or way of talking and so forth. However, the book of Revelation is an exception to the general rule of Bible interpretation in that Revelation is generally written overtly in symbolic or spiritual language dealing with beasts, marks, fish, locusts, the woman who flees into the wilderness, etc.

Symbolic language does *not* mean that it is not true, **literally true**, concerning some event in history and its spiritual significance. But **the symbol** does not have to be **physically** true. If Jesus says he is a door, that does not mean a physical door, or if He rules with a rod of iron that does not mean Jesus has to hold a rod of iron in His hand and hit people over the head with it, etc. In short, Revelation is a type of literature (that is largely metaphorical or symbolic language) that God chose to use to convey its message, but the message of Revelation and the interpretation of its symbols and metaphors should be done in terms of the larger points of history and in terms of the story of all history and all prophecy as laid out in the rest of the Bible.

The Larger Story of All Prophecy and All History
In a nutshell what is the larger story of all history? God created the "heavens and the earth" in six days and rested on the seventh. Presumably this means six 24 hour periods or six thousand years (if either can be made compatible with modern science). He created Adam and Eve, and they were deceived and tempted by Satan, and they disobeyed God in sin and died at that point spiritually speaking, thus all mankind after them has a fallen nature, and all are dead spiritually speaking in their trespasses and sins, and therefore all mankind needs the atoning sacrifice of Christ not just for their sin in Adam but for the particular sins of their own lives, and all mankind needs spiritual rebirth or regeneration that comes with accepting Christ as Lord and Savior.

All mankind is said to be **in Adam** (that is, fallen in sin by nature and actions as well as spiritually dead to God) or to be **in Christ**, that is, reborn and righteous saints with new hearts to God in Abba Father relationship and spiritual experience. (Romans 5 and Galatians 4 give a very clear statement of most of these points.)

After the fall of man in the Garden, time passes and God makes a covenant with Abraham whose faith God counted as righteousness. Abraham was justified by faith as Christians will be in Christ. And Abraham is to be the spiritual father of many nations. At the same time Abraham is to be the physical father of the Jewish people with whom God is in special covenant relationship, and God gives the Law to Moses for the Jewish people at Sinai. This Law is called the Old Testament or Old Covenant, and in Christ God makes a New Covenant for not only the Jewish people but for all mankind on Earth. The New Testament indicates though many Jewish people will become Christians, the Jewish people as a whole will not accept the New Covenant until the Kingdom Era comes on Earth in all its fullness. (See Romans 11.)

As is well-known the Jewish people did not accept Christ as the messiah because they were looking for a political messiah to do Just and Righteous government in Wisdom (as David and Solomon had done), and the promised messiah would do this not just in Israel but throughout the world in a promised Millennial Era in countless Old Testament prophecies concerning this coming time on Earth.

In truth, *if* Christ in the saints and the saints in Christ set up a world of Just and Righteous governments in a Judeo-Christian millennial era, that deed will fulfill the prophecies the Jews wanted for the Jewish messiah, *and* it will at the same time time prove that the Jewish messiah is Christ because it is Christ in the saints and the saints in Christ that eventually pull off what the Jewish people had wanted and expected from Jesus.

You might say, it just took Him 2000 years. I guess one could say Christ is a slow worker, *but* this is the overall story of prophecy that one needs to have in order to make all lesser prophecies fit into it.

Further, it means there will be a Church Age where the coming of the Kingdom of God on Earth is generally associated with the Church or what Augustine called the City of God, and there will also be a Kingdom Era that follows the Church Age. In a Kingdom Era we will see virtually all people on Earth come to Christ in Christian salvation where each will know the Lord from the least to the greatest. And, further, we will see Just and Righteous governments throughout the world. And Scripture seems pretty clear that demons and Satanic deception of the nations with Satan's false political ideologies will be bound for 1000 years. (See Revelation 20.)

Another Major Event of Prophecy: The Great Apostasy

The above general overview of history and prophecy allows one to interpret other significant and important prophecies fairly easily. The sign of the end of the age is given by Paul in 2 Thessalonians 2 specifically for this purpose. There must be the great "falling away" of the Church, sometimes called the Great Apostasy. Christian Liberalism of the Higher Critics, Harry Emerson Fosdick, and the mainline denominations is clearly the Great Apostasy. There is not even a maybe about this. Why?

If today's Christian Liberalism is not the Great Apostasy, the mainline churches would have to return to the faith and fall away yet again in order to fulfill the falling away prophecy, and that is almost certainly *not* going to happen, which means the mainline denominations returning to a Bible-based faith will mark the beginning of mankind's transition into the Kingdom Era.

Further, the Great Apostasy is by definition what Paul calls in 2 Corinthians 11 "another Jesus spirit" and "another Gospel," which is obviously a demonic "Jesus" spirit and a false Gospel of "doctrines of demons." Christian Liberalism has a Gnostic and utopian "Jesus" preaching an agape love as lawlessness, sometimes called "unconditional love" by Liberals. For the ancient Gnostic, as for the modern Liberal, the God of the Old Testament is a God of Justice, Righteousness, and Judgment, and therefore He is evil because He does not let everyone into heaven in what is known as universalism of unconditional love. And for the ancient Gnostic, as for the modern Liberal, the God of Jesus in the New Testament is supposedly a different "God" of unconditional love and universalism.

The new "Gospel" of the Great Apostasy is agape love as license or lawlessness, and it has a "Gospel" and demonic spirit of tolerance, if not outright indulgence and a "Gospel" of acceptance, inclusion, unity or oneness. This is clearly the false spirit of a false "Jesus" in the Laodicean church which thinks it is spiritually rich and in need of nothing when in fact it is poor, blind, wretched and naked, and the *real* Spirit of Jesus in not even in the church but standing outside knocking on the door to come in and have fellowship (spiritual experiences) with them. And when or if they open the door to the Jesus of Scripture, the mainline denominations in the Great Apostasy will return to the faith, Jesus, and Gospel of the Bible, which is a Good News that Jesus died on the Cross for our sins to reconcile us to God and not to reconcile us to each other as the Liberals teach. And the Liberals will then also return to the practice of moral virtue (as in the Two Great Commandments) as the point of the faith and not tolerance and unity.

Again, these transitions of the mainline denominations back to the Good News of salvation in Christ and of new Spiritual life in Christ will be the sign that we are transitioning into the prophesied Kingdom Era in the realm of religion, and it will be accompanied by a transition of the nations of the world into Just and Righteous government, the thing that the Jews were looking for in Jesus but did not get 2000 years ago.

The Man of Lawlessness
This touches on the second major aspect of the famous 2 Thessalonians 2 prophecy, which is "the man of lawlessness" presents himself "in the temple" deceiving many. The man of lawlessness is a political figure pretty clearly as Bible commentators have held from the earliest days of the Church, and "in the temple" means probably before the people of God who are the living temple of God and not in a rebuilt physical temple in Jerusalem.

And when the man of lawlessness presents himself before the people of God, there is great deception among the people, and Jesus says if possible this particular man of lawlessness would deceive even the very elect because his deception powers are so great. (See Matthew 24:24.)

Please note, this is the whole ball game because *all* **political figures who are humanist atheists or Liberals** do *not* believe in the moral Laws of Nature and of Nature's God of the Glorious Revolution or the American Revolution. A man of lawlessness is what is called a type in Scripture typology. **The spirit of lawlessness is the spirit of Antichrist**

throughout Scripture as in Matthew 7:23 where the practice of lawlessness is the standard of the Final Judgment. Lawlessness is opposed to righteousness (as in 1 Timothy 1:9).

Lawlessness is generally associated with wickedness, which has the connotation of twisted to the law as a wick in a candle is twisted fibers or threads. In fact, some New Testament translations interchange the words lawless and wicked. And as individual lawless or wicked people go there are many Antichrists says 1 John 2:18, but there is one final great lawless figure at the end of the Church Age.

The entire point of Liberalism and of humanism or atheism is that they both reject what is called the Higher Moral Law of God *and* the God that goes with that Higher Moral Law. If this is the case, this passage on the man of lawlessness in 2 Thessalonians 2 means today's entire Democratic Party in the US and today's entire Labour Party in the UK are in a spirit of lawlessness or so-called "anti-Christ" in rejecting the moral Laws of Nature and of Nature's God of Locke, Jefferson, and the American founders. And what is the "deception" of the man of lawlessness? The deception is that the man of lawlessness makes people think his in fact wicked lawlessness is a true moral high ground or true audacity of hope, etc.

In this context, a false Christ figure of lawlessness is called "anti-Christ" where anti means *both* against *and* false or counterfeit. That is to say, the lawless politician deceives many with a **counterfeit** message that is actually **opposed** to Christ, but it is often seemingly in the name of Christ (or there would be no deception), and this is the **political** parallel to the exact same situation in the **religious** condition of the Laodicean church, which has a false, even demonic, "Jesus" spirit that the Laodicean church thinks is the real thing, tragically, but in fact that spirit is as lawless as the political man of lawlessness.

Babylon and Mystery Babylon, the Harlot
In Revelation "Babylon" is generally accepted to be a one-world totalitarian and tyrannical government that wants to control everything we buy, sell, do, say or even think. All our actions and words are to be **marked** by this politically correct totalitarian humanism as is all our thought and thinking, or we suffer the unpleasant consequences from the Beast Babylon. And the economy is completely controlled by the one-world totalitarian and tyrannical government; say good-bye to free enterprise!

The mark of the Beast on our hands is the symbol for all our actions, and the mark on our foreheads is the symbol for all our thought. And, of course, socialism and hard communism openly advocate a command-and-control economy to do worldwide Social Justice wealth redistribution, totally eliminating free enterprise and capitalism. This is straight out of the book of Revelation, where one cannot buy or sell **anything** without "the mark of the Beast" of the one-world government controlling **all** economic transactions.

And, as is well-known among Bible commentators, the enabler of the political Beast Babylon (the one-world totalitarian government) is called Mystery Babylon or the religious harlot or the Whore of Babylon riding on the political Babylon Beast in Revelation 17.

Bible commentators commonly (and correctly in my opinion) see this religious Mystery Babylon to be doing a false one-world religion that says all religions worship the same God but by a different name. And lo and behold, **this is a central part of the teaching and belief of the Liberal apostate church of Laodicea**! And here we are!

This means the mainline denominations of today are the good ole Whore of Babylon as they advocate a lawless Gospel of tolerance and inclusion with a political and economic agenda of worldwide Social Justice, which is the exact same Socialist Justice agenda as the one-world socialist government of Beast Babylon.

The Beast controls all we buy, sell, do, say or even think in a bizarre totalitarian, tyrannical, and politically correct world. The Beast is clearly doing a worldwide command-and-control economy, which in our day is an evil worldwide socialism or Socialist "Justice." And all of this nonsense is to be taught worldwide in the politically correct schools as good, right and true! And, yet again, here we are!

One-World Government & One-World Religion
So, in the big picture all of this makes the central issues and problems of **Revelation** to be **one-world government** and **one-world religion**. There is little or no question or debate about this among conservative Bible scholars, and what do we know? **Globalism** in law, government, education, economics, and politics and **Christian apostasy** in religion are **the two great issues of our time!** Holy smoke, this is it!

Revelation is, it seems, happening all around us, without any question. However, the usual response one hears to this is we do not yet have the one-world government of Babylon to control everything we buy, sell, do, say or even think, but we are moving toward it. And we do not quite yet have an explicit one-world religion, as such. So, the argument goes we are not quite yet in the book of Revelation, but we are on the verge of it. However, this position is not correct.

If one does a good bit of research on the internet, one will find that the United Nations was actually established to set up a one-world socialist government to control worldwide everything we buy, sell, do, say or even think, and this is written into the founding documents of the United Nations, namely, the UN Charter and the Universal Declaration of Human Rights. And to top it all off all the nations of the world have pledged and committed themselves to fulfill **this founding agenda of the UN** in the coming years and indeed in the coming millennium.

And things are worse than this because the official World Council of Churches formed at the same time in 1948 was openly Liberal, that is, apostate, in its foundational beliefs in promoting the universal fatherhood of God and the universal brotherhood of man with a worldwide Social Justice agenda of the United Nations. This is not in dispute, and it is so much the case that the non-Liberal, traditional and conservative denominations openly refused to join the World Council of Churches.

So, Revelation is a done deal, period. It is like getting married. Once you say "I do," you're married, for better or worse. All the nations of the world said "I do" to the UN Charter and the Universal Declaration of Human Rights and to the UN's ultimate aims to control with time all we buy, sell, do, say or even think. Once this pledge and commitment was made, the prophecy of the Revelation Beast of Babylon was fulfilled. And the same goes for the mainline denominations saying "I do" to the World Council of Churches and its apostate one-world religion agenda and its faulty theology. The World Council of Churches is Mystery Babylon, the Whore of Babylon, and I can see no other way to view this, for better or worse. Wake up, smell the coffee.

Quite simply, the United Nations is, and is meant to be, and was founded to be an unelected, totalitarian and tyrannical one-world governmental authority to rule over all nations and to control everything we buy, sell, do, say or even think in worldwide socialist Social Justice and in worldwide socialist indoctrination called "education" and in politically correct speech, press, and religion, and all the nations of the world said, "I do." And here we are, obviously not a very good situation, but nonetheless this is all *very* clear fulfillment of almost all of Revelation **as past history**, no less.

But as the expression goes, "It ain't over till it's over" or as sometimes said of such situations, "It ain't over till the fat lady sings." And that would be Revelation 19, quite literally. Saddle up, saints! However, Revelation 19 is not talking about getting on literal horses, please.

Revelation 19: The Final Battle
The truth is today the only significant pushback to one-world government and one-world religion is by the "deplorables" (that is, traditional Christians) in political national sovereignty movements led by such figures as Donald Trump and Nigel Farage and led in religion by today's Evangelicals. We are not going to be coming from Heaven riding out of the clouds on physical horses, but rather this imagery means we

are not of this world but we are citizens of the household of God of Heaven (Ephesians 2:19) at least in the realm of the spirit, and we are doing God's will for Just and Righteous government and for true religion in Spirit and Truth as best we can. And we are in Christ, and Christ is in us, and Christ is riding point, no doubt about it. Christ is head of this army!

And in Revelation 19 there is a huge struggle or battle in the realm of the spirit, and the saints in Christ prevail and defeat the demonic forces of darkness, deception, evil and tyranny as well as the false light of politically correct one-world Social Justice government to control everything buy, sell, do, say or even think, and we defeat or expose the false light of one-world false religion worshipping demon spirits (no less) as supposedly the true God of Scripture, which is outrageous but the norm today in most of the mainline denominations.

In short, we the saints in Christ, we the so-called "deplorables," win the battle against one-world government and one-world religion says Revelation 19, and in Revelation 20 Satan is then bound in the bottomless pit to "deceive the nations no more" for a thousand years. It sounds like Satan is going to cool his jets a bit in the prison of a black hole for a thousand years, tough luck for him. He has it coming no doubt. Presumably Satan in this context represents all demons.

Game over, we win

We the saints then restore the apostate churches and win the whole world to Christ in Christian salvation, and we then set up Just and Righteous nations worldwide in peace and prosperity, and this will fulfill all the major Kingdom Era prophecies, and then each shall know the Lord from the least to the greatest, and the knowledge of God will fill the whole earth as waters fill the sea. And, in the realm of the spirit, Revelation 20 says the great saints of the past will be with us (though in spirit only presumably) for the whole thousand years sharing, as vindicated inspirations, in our triumph and success. Amen.

===

Other booklets on the Reign of Christ in this UNDERSTANDING Series:

UNDERSTANDING Prophecy Fulfillment:
The Great Apostasy, Babylon, Mystery Babylon & the Reign of Christ

This little booklet gives an overview of the central major prophecies concerning the possible soon coming Reign of Christ. Specifically these are the prophecies of the Great Apostasy, Babylon, Mystery Babylon, and the man of lawlessness. These prophecies are seen as fulfilled in the false millennial visions of Marx and of the New World Order of UN Agenda 21 and Agenda 2030 and in the Liberal World Council of Churches.

UNDERSTANDING All Bible Prophecy:
Genesis to Revelation

This booklet holds that all prophecy should be interpreted in terms of the larger story of the Bible and the larger story of the Christian cosmology from the Creation to the Final Judgment, and this is especially the case for the book of Revelation.

UNDERSTANDING Globalism:
What is the "New World Order"?

This booklet looks at what "globalism" is generally and at the related topic of a "New World Order" that actually has **very** specific definitions and formulations that are often not well-known.

UNDERSTANDING Revelation 19:
Victory over One-World Government and One-World Religion

Revelation 19 though very controversial is actually very straightforward. The saints in a Marriage Supper of the Lamb move into a new more mature, intimate, and complete relationship with Christ, and then the saints in Christ and Christ in the saints completely and totally defeat the evils of one-world government and one-world religion. Simple enough when you get right down to it.

UNDERSTANDING Statesmanship
Classical Justice *versus* Social Justice

Probably no two notions are more misunderstood as well as more necessary to understand in our time than classical Justice and Social Justice. This booklet looks at the history of these two terms and how one stands for the Justice of statesmanship for doing the common good and the other for the injustice of special interest groups and wealth redistribution as a false human right for economic equality.

UNDERSTANDING Alternative Political Universes:
The Natural Revelation & Self-Evident Truths

For some folks as Jefferson and the American founders, the Natural Law or so-called Higher Moral Law is a self-evident truth, but for others with a reprobate mind and no common sense, this is not the case at all. These modern-day people who have lost their common sense are just as the ancient Epicureans (atheist hedonists) while modern-day Liberals are just as ancient Gnostics with their false enlightenment and false morality. Understand these things, and you will pretty well understand Alternative Political Universes.

UNDERSTANDING Illegal Immigration:
The Wall and All It Stands For

"The Wall" of Donald Trump stands for many larger issues from exposing hypocrisy among professional politicians to ending globalism, open borders, and the often total lawlessness of our time. Lawlessness of the Liberal and atheist-humanist is, in fact, the spirit of anti-Christ.

UNDERSTANDING The Whole Counsel of the Kingdom:
The Central Message of Jesus and Paul

Both Jesus and Paul preached a Whole Counsel of the Kingdom message, but this is not a generally well-known truth. This booklet looks at the concept of a Whole Counsel of the Kingdom Christianity and what it entails, namely, true worship of God in Spirit and Truth as well as Just and Righteous government.

UNDERSTANDING Spiritual Warfare:
Satan as a Roaring Lion

Scripture tells us that Satan goes about like a roaring lion seeking whom he may devour, but this is generally not a very understood warning, and tragically many people, if not devoured completely, get an arm or leg eaten (so to speak). To be forewarned is to be forearmed. This booklet deals with ways to recognize and deal with demons.

===

All of the above booklets are part of a series on key issues of our time on the Reign of Christ at
www.ashiningcityonahill.org
www.reignofchrist.org

All of the above booklets are put together is a single **Volume I** called

UNDERSTANDING
The Reign of CHRIST:
The One Big Issue of Our Time
Volume I

This Volume I of all the above booklets together as well as all of the above booklets separately are available at **amazon.com**